Walls of Silk

Love is a bitter rose beautifully painful and painfully beautiful.
- ANR
Whether you were a nerd or a drop out either way high school sucked. – ANR

 This book is dedicated to my family and to all those who support and believe in me and to all the artists and dreamers.

Thank you God Copyright 2013 ©

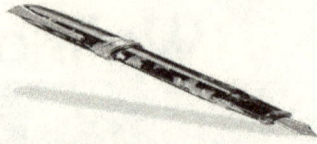

Contents:

Lazy Bed

Seduced

A letter from Mistress Nicole to her slave

Here for Artist

Thinker

Revealed

Liar's Question

Love letter to the moon

Days

Joy and Singing

Walls of Silk

Inhale

Betrayed

Numb

Peace

Regret

Little Girl

A Woman

Goodbye

Train Changer

Dear Missing Piece

Gypsy

Raindrops

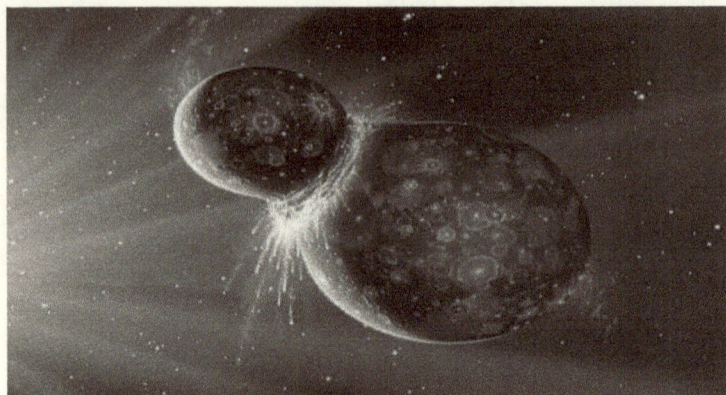

Cosmic Orgasm

You are the sky. I am the stars. High into the heavens still we reach farther. We are love astronauts planning explorations. Let's go out of space and play with stardust.

The flames from our desire burn bright. They bend the laws of gravity. The sparkle in your eyes ignites the fire in my mind. Our skin glows passion red. We make warm kindling conversations. Our lips unite the universe.

Human satellites detect our frequency and they listen anxiously. I see your planet. I feel your big dipper deep inside my constellation. What a cosmic orgasmic sensation. You are my solar eclipse.

Nature takes its course and orbital shifting force our planets to collide creating a cataclysmic explosion inside. We glide into the twilight. This is galactic ecstasy, me next to you and you next to me. I am your moon ,put your ring around me.

We can't stop this rocket now, its already too far gone. I see the light getting brighter. I feel the heat getting hotter. The temperature's rising all the way up.

Shivers start moving down our spines where the planets align. Your warm delight flows through me cosmicly. I am an open channel born.

Sweet Milky Way, yes this cosmic orgasm has captured me. I day dream. You night dream. We both scream. Late nights lead to early morning satisfying the dawn with our cosmic orgasm.

11/28/2013

I'm sorry I can't look at you and smile even when I see you smiling. That smile is just too hard to fake, too painful to pretend. I've tried. They say smiling is a reflex. I guess mine is broken.

I'm sorry I do not know you. Sorry you aren't familiar to me. I feel totally disconnected and I wish things weren't this way. I'm sorry I look in the mirror and do not see you. I look at pictures and do not recognize you. Sadly we are strangers and I'm not sure I can do anything about it. I'm sorry we were never introduced, never given an opportunity to get to know each other.

But tragically time has passed now and we are both different people.

I know you don't know me and I don't know you but let me say this, please take care of yourself. You are the only you you have.

Your face tells a familiar story. You look lost inside a strange body, empty of an existence and painfully confused .You look like you feel unloved and unworthy. I know that look and it will never change their minds. I know that feeling and it will never be comfortable.
I'm so sorry. I'm sorry I don't know you. Sorry we never met. Sorry I never played with you. Sorry I couldn't save you. I'm sorry we were never children.

Written by Alisha Ratliff as anr 11/21/13

I do not like mischief but mischief likes me. He looks for me to play hide and seek, we do and inevitably I always find myself in trouble. He changes the game to tag and without warning I am it again.

Mischief loves deceiving me. He wears disguises subtlety. He changes daily drastically. He is tall and short depending on when. He is kind sometimes I think he's my friend.

He has blue eyes and brown eyes sometimes. He is handsome and tasty in the morning. Sometimes he taste like strawberry and sometimes he tastes like cinnamon and sometimes we have fun.

Mischief likes opportunity. He's a spontaneous character randomly. He wakes me up for breakfast at midnight. We avoid the stove but not disaster and after we eat he takes my sleep.

We play more games then watch TV. We get into more trouble unexpectedly. I get blamed and he goes free. I do not like mischief but mischief likes me.

SCREAM

I can't hold this energy in me anymore. It's slowly seeping out finding its way to the nearest exit. My vocal chords volunteer suddenly.

I must, I must I trust you understand. I have to scream. I'm full and overflowing. I feel it sliding out,gliding on this shout. My lips just can't stay sealed it's stronger than my will. The feelings deep inside have no place to hide. Here comes my release, it builds up constantly. I have to scream. My breath starts slow then speeds when I don't get what I need. I try with all my might but I just can't win this fight. I feel the loud roar coming, it's moving in my stomach. My hands cover my mouth but then I lose control and my hand loses its hold and then I just explode. I hope you can forgive me. I pray you understand, join me if you dare, but I have to scream.

July 11, 2013

Rain

Sexy rain, steamy rain you seduce me drop by drop. I watch you outside my window wetting everything you touch. I want to go outside and let you wet me and saturate me. I am memorized.

Soothing and calm you flirt with me enticing me into your bed. I am inclined to come. Erotic rain, stormy rain you turn me on. You caress my thoughts like gentle lovers kisses there can never be too many.

You flood my skin with devoted passion . The sun's passion to shine through thick clouds. I am aroused watching your hard downfall.

Your flashes of lightening trace my body casting my wet dripping shadow. Your deep thunder whispers to me all that I desire. You are my desire.
You undress me with each crash buttons, zippers and strings. You smile bidding me under your sky. You wink inviting me under your blanket. I surrender. Don't stop falling yet. Pour more. Day until night sweet shower consume me.
Written by Alisha Ratliff as ANR

seamless SM

11/21/2013

Seamless it seems you make no sense. You bring no string to connect anything. You are perfectly consistent sometimes.

You are bottled confusion, a smokeless vapor. You are carbonated crazy. You are seams with no stitching on legless pants. You are walking contradiction.

You are corners without walls and skinless fruit. You are seasons unchanging. You are winter in sunshine and Christmas in June, timeless and new. You are hot snow.

You are a lecture about speeches given on handouts. You are digital paper.
You leave an iron's wrinkle. You are straight around the edges. You are chairs without seats.

You are a sand less nude beach for naked people with clothed minds. It seems you are everywhere. You are army ants surrendered. You are uncommon sense.

You are a picture with no paint, a book with no pages. You are the stairs to nowhere.

You are days inside an hour lost in lovers eyes. You are the absence of time. You are sin and happiness in a fallen man high.

You are bliss and folly on a plate of lies. You are the cup of logic spilled. You are the loneliest crowd. You are seamless.

You are not enough to know that you are everything.

Night Awake

2/24/2013

Late at night I lay awake. I find myself slumber less in the darkness. I contemplate my life in the silence of the moon. The life I have lived and the one of my dreams. I compare their similarities and differences. They are vast and I am sad.

I scrutinize my actions the things I have done and failed to do, that moment I did not smile at a stranger. The choices I made both good and bad saying yes instead of no, saying no instead of yes. It becomes difficult to lie still but I pay conscious what it is owed and wish for sleep.

I stare deep into the abyss until reality becomes clear. I appear in the dark as I am blind to the light. Beautiful, powerful, and graceful. Here I live the life of my dreams. I fly high into the stars becoming unfamiliar with earth and its holding. I am free of any destructive gravity.

I excel above my inhibitions. I emerge as my higher self, true, alive and full of reality. I find myself in the sacred place complete. Surprisingly, I find that I am enough and have been all along and I do not wish for sleep.

Surrender

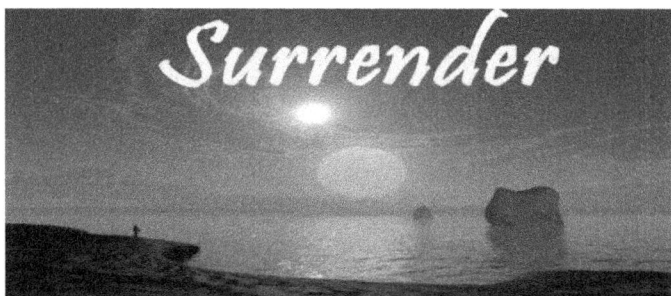

Brave Surrender

My heart is breaking and my knees are shaking. My breathe is shallow. My pulse is weak and my mouth can hardly speak. My voice is faintly cracking from the true love I've been lacking.

Can anyone see my S.O.S.? Can anyone hear my silent screaming? Can anyone feel my constant beating? Can anyone check my internal bleeding?

My insides are out. My upside is down. Will anyone answer my needy knocking or dock the time of loss I'm clocking?
My desperate desires go unfulfilled. I suffocate in my tear stained pillow.

Asking, needing begging, longing, wanting nothing more than to be loved. Not Fucked, Loved. (Yes) – 2nd Not lusted, Loved. (yes) 2nd Just Loved.2nd (yes) Is that too much?

Can I be me entirely and let you see without fear you'll flee.
You tell me (yes. I want to love you.)2nd
But how does a broken heart believe? How does a fragile mind conceive? How does a suppressed soul receive? How do I want what I need?

Internally I'm seeking you. Externally I appear to be present though absent and empty inside. You still say (yes, I want to love you, let me.) 2nd

Passionately I crave you and what you are offering. Desperately I need you and what you are giving. You reach for me consistently love.(yes, take me) extending your warm hand.

I accept you now with brave surrender. I trust you and breathe you with brave surrender. I cast aside my fears for you.
If only I can be loved (yes) 2nd and free with you for an hour or a day. Dare I dream forever.

Giving myself to you, all that I am and all that I have. Love (yes) 2nd I will let you love me and save me with brave surrender. I will. I am deeply yours without hesitation or reservation with brave surrender love. 2nd (finally yes).
Written by; Alisha Ratliff as anrcandy 2012 Duet 2 person performance 2nd person – Love speaking

Horizon

I have found forever love inside the bright horizon. He has captured me sweetly. We are lovers and our bodies orbit likes seasons. We are joined in eternity crest to crown like roots to soil. Earth defines the sky, clouds complete the rainbow and our love welcomes the moon. We bask in its silver glow.
I stand before him his exotic queen graceful and radiant. He undresses me slowly and crowns me light. He calls me beautiful and I am pleased as he kneels before me. He is strong, lasting and sure.

He wraps his arms me gently. I am his desire and he is mine. We are curious trees dancing to the wind song. We spend long hours running familiar fingers over naked thighs for the first time. We swim in a sweet river of endless passion and go under for hours. We reemerge satisfied.
 We are royal mountains, connected by the setting sun. We are breathless stars shining over silk shadows.

We drink from the cup of devoted pleasures and close our eyes. We brace for advanced orgasms and taste their juices. We awaken drunk with folly and follow its lead, hearts fully engaged, thirsty for life unborn, and treasures undiscovered. We bathe in loyal ocean waves and spend all afternoon exploring the luminance of an imagined heaven.

11/23/2013

Heart First, Head Second

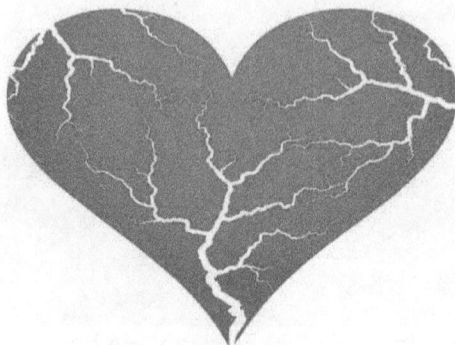

I tried to stop loving you. How I tried, but my heart wouldn't. I wanted to be done with you honestly. I spent countless hours keeping busy, endless days and various methods trying to rid any sign of you from my mind but my heart found a way to beat for you and bleed for you. It seemed so reasonable to just let go of you and your toxic poison but I couldn't.

I swear I did not want to love you. I willed myself not to. I knew you were dangerous and cruel yet I found myself loving you anyhow.

My mind knew you were no good. As wicked as it seemed you were a nightmare instead of a dream. Painful to the bone, your betrayal was lethal imprinted on my brain, yet my heart found a way to love you against advice.

Desperately I tried to convince myself to pick up the wreckage and move on, assuring myself I would be smarter and more cautious next time. I pondered the tears. I pondered the years. I counted the cost of all that I had lost and still my heart found a way to bleed for you again.

I tried to deny you with all of my might but I was forced against my will. It defied all logic. My mind couldn't believe it, and still my heart conceived it. I found a way to love you heart first head second.

July 11, 2013

Resurrect !

Resurrect young soul and live the reality your ancestors could only dream. Arise from your enslaved slumber. Ignite from your drunken stupor, your induced comma Resurrect young soul and ride your maverick achieve the orgasmic.

Awaken from your false illusion brave solider. Fight for your cause. Rule justly great king. Judge fairly in your courts.

Resurrect young soul and be devoted to the duty of being free. It is great heroism to be yourself wholly and complete.

Freedom is not given but taken. It is not born but made. Resurrect young soul and be proud. You are called to stand bold and tall.

Dispatch briskly to make your mind available to knowledge, your soul available to wisdom, and your heart available to love. Advance on the first wave to free your inner slave. Resurrect young soul. Alert the spirit of the masses to resurrect.

Young soul live, young soul give, young soul thrive, earn your place in the race to truly be alive. Read it and shout it, tell all about it. Many are dead who weren't warned ahead.

Today is your third day, now is your Easter. Live dreams that breathe, hopes that believe, and destinies that conceive. Take opportunities to seek, your longings and needs find fulfillment indeed. The power to choose is yours to use or lose.

Young soul resurrect! 12/20/12

Written by Alisha Ratliff as anr 11/21/2013

Here is my Proclamation I make to you a
solemn vow tomorrow will be different and
every day after that because today I
forgive you. yes I choose to. I forgive you
for lying to me I know now you couldn't
tell me the truth, you didn't know it and
you did not recognize it.

 I forgive you for insulting me and
embarrassing me telling me I was worthless
and useless and unlovable. You couldn't
appreciate my worth. You didn't know who I
was. I forgive you.

I forgive you for abandoning me and leaving
me for dead and empty without explanation,
swimming in the sea of bitter tears and
growing fears. I forgive you for leaving me
feeling rejected and broken. You couldn't
stay, and I forgive you for that too.

 I forgive you for breaking my heart and
choosing her instead of me. I forgive you
for coming home late and leaving for work
early and for turning your phone on
vibrate. I forgive you for lying to me and
falling asleep with not so much is a good
night because you at spent your time and

energy on her. You couldn't have choose me. I wasn't that easy.

I forgive you for packing up my things along with yours and taking them, and for taking my body my love my loyalty, my energy, my home, my joy, my passion my sacrifice my beauty for granted and for throwing them all in the trash. I forgive you throwing me away. You didn't know what you had.

I forgive you, be at peace. Tomorrow will be different but not because I forgive you tomorrow will be different because I forgive me for allowing you to use, abuse and mistreat me.
I forgive me for not knowing who I was and seeking validation in someone else who was not even valid. I forgive myself for believing your lies and seeking happiness in your arms and identity in your eyes.
And so know that today is done and its troubles too and tomorrow will be different and you will never have the opportunity to hurt me again because we are both identified and forgiven.

Chapter New

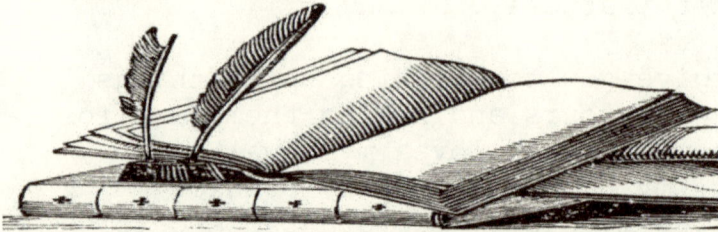

11/21/13

Today is a new day, a new chapter in this book we call humanity. There is a new sun shining over everything and everyone every tree and every sea. The darkness of yesterday is buried in the light of today. Each painful moment is carefully wrapped in the cloth of sleep like mummies in a tomb. It is not yet realized what is written for us today, but there is new light and opportunity. There is the chance to live again.

Today is a new reason to smile. New grass is growing, new hair is too, new strangers are becoming friends, old friends are becoming family. Wives are becoming mothers and husbands are becoming fathers, sisters are becoming siblings. Today is a new chapter in this book we call family.

Some broken things are still breaking, some broken things are mending. Boys are becoming men. Men are becoming soldiers, soldiers are becoming veterans and some women are becoming superwomen. Today is a new chapter this book we call love.

Writers are becoming authors and actors are becoming stars. New chapters are being written. Loves are lost and found. Some lives are being given and some are being

taken through birth and death and the space
in between in this book we call destiny.

What was old is new and what was new is
used like cars and shoes. Vintage is novel.
What is moving lies still. What is working
finds rest, what is resting finds purpose.
Who is called hears his name. Today is a
new chapter in the book we call redemption.
Today is a new day. It is present without
past or future, and someone will meet
strangers and find love. Someone will find
mystery and revelation. Someone will know
familiar confusion. Someone will see God
and evil. Others will feel pleasure and
pain. Today is a new chapter in this book
we call surrender.
Today is a new day, someone will dare to
dream,dare pick up a pen and write a new
chapter in the book we call me.

Solace Sweeps

By:Alisha Ratliff as ANR

I find solace between the tide's rise and fall, when the twilight darkens and freedom calls. I relax my hand along the damp sea sand, where the little waves roll and crash. I find solace in indented footprints far along the beaches shore I crave for more.

I find solace in the sweeping motion of the midnight wind blowing my hair aside, I breathe in deep where the kingdom of the heavens hasten to hear my morning wishes and serenity is not the enemy. I find solace where the inviting sky holds its diamonds safely kept. Where the morning sun breaks through the moon's stall and day returns. I find solace where the waving palms give rest and shade. The rolling sea washes over me and generously offers fresh eyes and renewal for my weary mind. Every lie is washed away.

I find solace where I am surrounded by the beauty of the deep blue calm. Pain and chaos vanish in the distance. False screams of rejection are silenced forever carried away on waves or serenity. Truth unfolds its glorious wonder and I am crowned with goodness. Fresh awareness brings clarity and understanding elevating my mind above the harmful debris. Every constraint loosens its hold. I am feed by the fruit of evening and quenched by its sweet juices.

I find solace where Wet bliss follows warm kisses smoothly transitioning me from ecstasy to reality until I see they are one in my conscious state. A safe abode solemn and departed where solace sweeps between the tides rise and fall.

Happy Accidents

Written by Alisha Ratliff as ANR 4/3/13

There are these happy accidents that occur when fortunately unaware. When instinctive decisions are made and spontaneous impulses are obeyed. When time is lost and feelings are dazed. There are these happy accidents when we find ourselves living the reality of our fantasies.

When moonlight collides with sunrise, and two hearts understand the language of silence. There are these happy accidents when a secret code unlocks pleasures undiscovered. When two smiles become fated laughter united.

There are these happy accidents when fears fade like memories and inhibitions dissolve like snowflakes, and calm coherence has no interference.

There are these happy accidents that remain and give way to lullaby kisses and romantic transmissions. When careful star gazing reveals the innocence of the moon and the beauty of the midnight sky.

When love making is warm intimate clothed conversation and naked foreplay is beautiful and mysterious. When stars comfortably change positions and heighten our senses.

There are these happy accidents when natural chemistry flows deep in the absence of sleep and a sweet connection builds warm security inside accepting arms. When passion fills a relentless heart.

There are these happy accidents when satisfied lovers surrender to orgasmic slumber and find morning the same. There are these happy accidents when we realize we have been favorably captured by love and its consuming power.

the happy accident

Snow

Why do you come so frequently and in such great quantity? For me you come inconveniently snow! Your heavy wet slush gets in my way. You cover the roads and slow down traffic and in some cases create disaster.

How cold you are as you fall to the ground accumulating inches all around. I bundle in layers to keep out your cold but you're just too much truth be told.

Sweaters and gloves seem to do no good even next to the fireplace burning with wood. I cannot stand to pull out my shovel, freezing my fingers is just too much trouble. You stick to the trees, you stick to the streets. You stick to the cars and even my feet.

When winter is over I am so glad goodbye snow so long at last.

Written by Alisha Ratliff as ANR 5/15/13

Deities

Written by Alisha Ratliff as anr 8/11/2013

We are little deities filled with power divine. We are god and man mysteriously. What blessed bliss you and I are god. We were favorably chosen the children of light.

We inhale eternity and exhale time. Some gods reign by day. They are suns. Others rule by night. They are stars. Each god and goddess are small yet significant sovereignly born to a lesser heaven.

We are mostly unaware of our supernatural nature robed in the human condition. We have free will and choice, what a gift. We love and cry and bleed, we sin and give life. We are guarded by angels and despised by demons.

We pass like seasons, winters of pain and punishment, summers of goodness and pleasure, springs of laughter and children and falls of peace and change. Both male and female we were predetermined and betrothed for greatness and wonder.

We were created sacred beings of love, formed of dirt and sky and there we shall return spirits of immortality and grace.

JustKnow

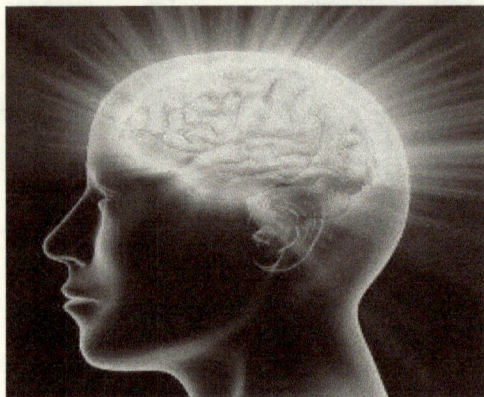

8/9/2013

I love you. I really do and I hope you believe me one day, no I pray you know it now. I love you the best way I can, the only way I know how.

The more I learn the better I promise to love you, but until then just know that I want what is best for you. I want your happiness and safety, just know that I want you to be free and secure. I want you be yourself above all.

Just know that I pray for you always that God protect you and guide you and make you great. Just know that when I am not with you I am thinking of you constantly and I want to be with you.

Just know I want to give you all that I have and that be enough.

You see it's really a long short story of why we are apart. The common story of a scared insecure girl learning to be a woman without a father and no real instructions on how to be a mother.

The familiar story of a girl who had no childhood to call her own, a girl who struggled to smile.

And so the decision was not easy but I chose not to hand down to you generational garbage that would steal your identity, desperate insecurities that would leave you vulnerable, loveless lies that would leave you empty, Shame that would make you feel unlovable, painful secrets that would make you feel unworthy and deficiencies of every kind.

No I want better for you I want you to have life!
And so as painful as it may be that we are not together now just know I am with you, and at every bed time I am reading you a story and tucking you in. I am with you every morning helping you get ready for school and sharing breakfast and smiles.

I laugh with you and cry with you, I eat with you and play with you. I rejoice with you and I send you kisses. I give you warm secure hugs everyday.

So as impossible as it seems just know that I love you and I hope that one day you will be proud to call me your mom.

Come

Written by Alisha Ratliff as anr 11/22/2013
Come holy lover and save me from myself. Extend your hand of redemption. I am yours and I seek no other. Cast out my fears and restore my joy. Your word is enough.

I rejoice at your footsteps. Let us feast on mercy at the table of passion and remember no more our separation. Let us drink wine and be merry again.
My love, hold me tight in your arms and do not let go. Let us find sun light and warmth in each others eyes once more.

My body is yours and your body is mine. Let us do as we desire. We are one body beautiful. Let us stand in naked truth and consummate our love. May we lie on the bed of Grace guilty.

May you never leave my side. Oh come holy lover let us embrace eternity again!

Dear Daughter,

You are so beautiful. What an amazing woman you have become. You are all grown up now. I wish that I had been there to watch you transform from a caterpillar so that I could fully appreciate the magnificent butterfly before me now. You have spread your wings and forged your own way.

I am proud of all you have become. I am honored to see you fly so gracefully.

Regretfully I could not be the father you needed nor give you the love and nourishment you deserved. I am deeply sorry I hurt you, and I did not protect you. I am sorry I was not there.

But here I am fortunate, that you have graciously landed on a branch of my favorite tree as if the winds of destiny lead you to me and God somehow favored me to partake in this incredible miracle.

This moment with you is my salvation, this second to have second chance is the redemption I do not deserve, and I repent. I love you my daughter with all of my heart and soul for all the hours and days and minutes remaining in my old age. I love you. I prayed for mercy and I have found it.

Written by: Alisha Ratliff as herself 11/1/2013
Inspired piece

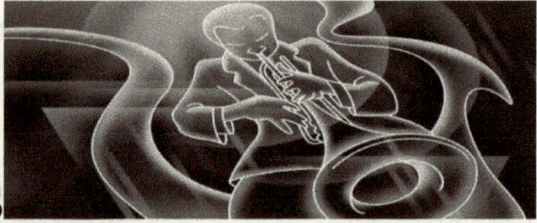

JazzSongs

Written by Alisha Ratliff as anr 8/16/13

I love to sing jazz songs at the top of my lungs. The rhythm gets into me and takes me to the clouds. I close my eyes and sing each raspy note in perfect pitch.

I am as rebellious and happy as jazz itself.I sing each key alphabetically until that soulful sound rings freedom loud.

I groove along until every word flows from my lips like a sultry river down a stream of excited ears. Jazz is my style. I wear it in my hair and in my smile.

I feel it in my fingers and toes. I feel it all over me. Jazz runs through my veins.

Each song tells a story. Each instrument plays its part recounting an adventure.

My lips are a jazz band unrehearsed. Love is my collaborator. I sing with the saxophone until his brass takes my breath and fills my lungs with righteous sound.

I strum the steamy guitar until his chords wash away time. I vibrate with music, it moves up my spine. My hands can't be still, neither can my knees. The trombone takes me on his roller-coaster.

I rock the base up to the stars and he rocks me. We rock steady unpredictably. I tickle the ivory keys carefully. They know my spots, and they tickle me.

I beat the sassy drum into sweet submission. The tempo fuels my blood. It makes my hips sway sideways.

I love to sing jazz songs at the top of my lungs until the neighbors join me in the streets to celebrate and we dance all night.

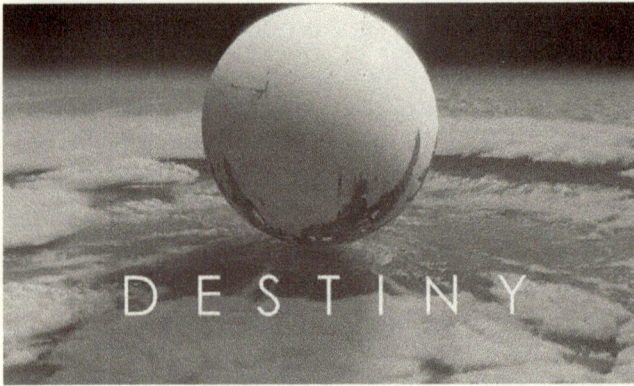

DESTINY

God,

Help me pursue my destiny and search with all my might. Give me courage to stand before my enemies, Make me ready to fight.

Show me how to give it life and nourish it from within. Teach me how to live out my destiny before I reach my end.

Show me where to walk the path to who I'm supposed to be. Let me dream with confidence comfortably being me.

Give me a sign you hear my prayers. God let me earn my destiny.

Written by Alisha Ratliff as ANR 7/15/2013

Vacancies of the Heart

A mass of constructed flesh lies in the cold alone worn out, torn out and barely beating, skipping the beats that were too painful to take. It couldn't.
This heart lies in broken pieces left by all who once called it home, vacant, bleeding out, crying out, even dying out. It seems love don't live here anymore and did not leave it's forwarding address.

Love is gone taken back by all the people who did not give it unconditionally, leaving this heart grieving and this soul in mourning struggling to regain some regularity.
They did not see this fragile flesh is more than a pumping machine. It is more than a metaphoric utopia where affections are exchanged. This heart stores many issues deep within its aching tissues.
Written by Alisha Ratliff as anr 7/15/2013

Lazy Bed

Today I decided to stay in bed. Stay warm and comfortable with the covers over my head.

I sleep then wake for lunch and a shower. I write some poetry then nap another hour. I read a book while eating my snack and when I'm done, I lay down and relax.

I put on my PJs and daydream some more. I close my eyelids and start to explore.
I make my dinner then back to bed again.
Today I was lazy and my bed was my friend.

June 18, 2013

Seduced

Written by : Alisha Ratliff as ANR

Seduction was a journey. The trip was bitter sweet. The ride was intoxicating. The road was irresistible. I tried my best to hold still to good character. I held to my morals like a drunk to his favorite bottle containing its final sip, firm yet casual. My conscious asked for permission to move. I granted it. It asked for permission to breathe. I inhaled. The signs were subtle. I watched my standards slowly become indecent like clothes falling to the floor during an erotic strip tease. Warm sultry whispers melted away any trace of self-control like ice cubes in a glass of sweet tea on a hot summer day. My will faded quickly like the ground fades into the distance from an airplane window as it ascends.

 Rules seemed more like suggestions for conduct to be considered rather than obeyed. My thoughts surrendered, my body followed. The objects of my affection came into view. Fantasy became reality and I begged for no escape. Happiness came in threes. My lovers held my hands and we danced.

We gave deep stares and passionate kisses forgetting our witnesses. Every perfect pleasure took possession of my senses. I saw the colorful beauty of body curves. I heard the joy in my lovers' laughter. I felt the degrees of heat rise. Happiness came in threes again.

Time stopped, my fears melt into my lover's eyes. Temptation gripped my body tightly and consumed me with bliss. Lust threw me on the bed slipping past conscious filters sending shock waves through my soul. I tried with all might but I lost the battle. Her lips lead me, his tongue guided me, both welcomed me into ecstasy.

Multiple orgasms escaped me before hours could be counted. My lips sang the sweet song of satisfaction. I was over taken by the no I kept saying yes to. I was fearlessly seduced.

A letter from Mistress Nicole to her slave,

You have been cosmically favored and afforded the great privilege to be my slave. You are not worthy of me yet but I will give you a chance. Here are your instructions. Your sole existence is for my satisfaction. Starting now you must obey me and do all that I command. Your every breath is to bring me pleasure and give me all that I desire.

You are my property. Your body is mine. Subject yourself and worship me. I am your supreme goddess.

Humble yourself now. Bow down and kiss my feet. You do not have permission to look at me or speak unless I give it. You are my slave. Say it every day. You are spellbound and weak under my control. You find me sexy, amazing and desirable. You want me but you must resist.

I will not tolerate insubordination. I will punish you immediately. I will chain and gag ball you. You will spend the night in my cage of hell naked. You will receive 50 lashes or as many as I like until I am satisfied.

I am your royal queen and you will bring me flowers whenever because I say so. You will kneel in my presence. You will address me "All great and beautiful mistress I am unworthy of you. How may I serve you?"

Close your eyes train your thoughts to me. I will reward your loyalty and obedience with great pleasure as any good Mistress would. If you earn it I will give you my collar and put my leash on you and take you for a walk.

Mistress Nicole

5/4/2013

Here for Artist

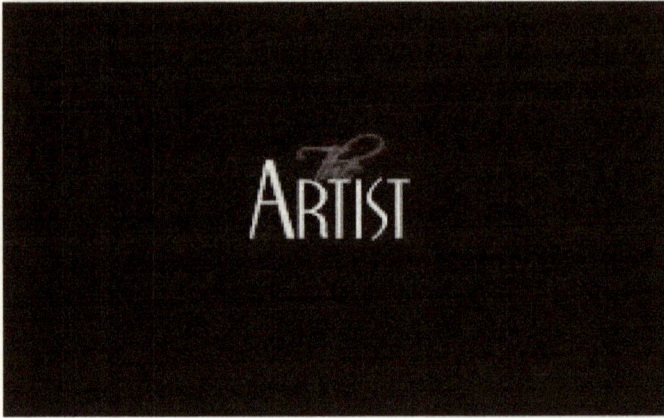

We are here to commune as artist. The brave faces of truth seekers and heart bleeders, the lovers of freedom. I invite you to join us.

We are here at this blessed table to sup and dine on what is truly divine, the creations of imaginations born in the mind.

To climb the tree of truth and eat of its fruits. We are hungry for life without limits. We ready for adventures untold. We eat at the banquet of dreams, the all you can taste feast of the arts. Dancers tickle our tongues.

We sing with the creators. We think with the inventors. We paint with the painter's. We write the writers. We are all one.

We fill our cups with laughter from above. Come, let us drink from the wells of passion and share their thirst quenching powers with the world. All who are childlike will find bliss.

We are here to plant in the garden of Eden with those who carry the seeds of eternity. We sow with them and breathe deep winds.

 Let us exalt the hidden voices and dirty our hands with thanksgiving and freedom.
July 31, 2013

Thinker

I saw the thinker and I thought what must he be thinking? Deep in contemplation lost, conscious or daydreaming? To sit and think the thoughts that passed, the one that came and went, must have taken hours to think the time he spent.

And from those thoughts came some conclusions and still more questions too. I think the thinker had to sit with so much thinking to do. And so his hand rose to his chin to keep his head in place, in case his brain were to expand from thinking out of space.
And now I sit and join the thinker thinking the thoughts that come and sitting still I contemplate where did these thoughts come from?
7/28/13

Revealed

Written by Alisha Ratliff as ANR 5/2/2013

I am freedom dawning in the new moon, peaking effortlessly in the glory of its shining. Graceful and small. I am revealed. A calm dangerous storm crashing quietly without warning. Pure spirit taking on flesh, acquiring time. Breathing deep, laughing hard, loving passionately, crying solemnly, living intentionally. I am revealed.

I am the sun's desire to rise and shine each morning, inviting the world to wake for a new day.Bright and consuming. I am revealed. A ball of blazing fire scorching forest, burning skin, warming hearts, melting lies.

I am water's will to flow and form intrepid waves creeping into midnight. Beaming and moving forward without cessation. I am mysterious energy rustling under currents. Overcoming as I go. True self persisting as an immortal star. I am a sweeping wind growing new trees and blowing dead leaves, first raging them calm. I am the singing field bringing lilies with each breeze. I am powerful and substantial when I am

revealed.

Liar'sQuestion

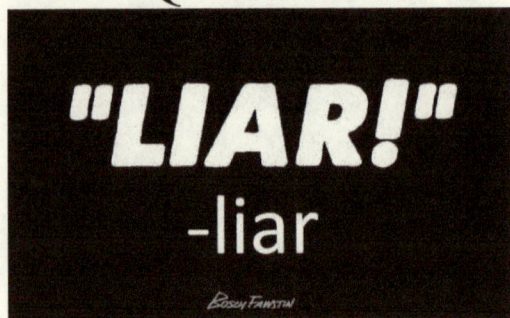

"LIAR!"
-liar

Boson Fanstin

11/22/2013

Why do you talk about me? Why am I on your
mind? What makes me relevant to you?

Why am I trending in your list of current
events? Why do I make your headlines? I'm
curious, why you care about my clothes or
my shoes you have not walked a mile in
them.

Why do you think about me? Does it really
fascinate you to know when I will be where?
Do you also have plans to be there? Why
must you know what I'll be doing? Are you
taking the same course I plan on pursuing?

Why do you need to know my status so bad?
If am married or single? Is it your
concern? Does it drive you mad? Do you care
either way if I am happy or sad?

Why is my pleasure your prerogative? Does
it excite you to know whether my lover is
male or female or both? If we make love?
How often? how good? How many times we
orgasm? And what's our favorite position?

It's plenty, its good we definitely do. Now I'm curious what about you?

I'd love to why you feel lead to lie. I honestly don't have a clue. Why do you care about me at all? I'm sure you'd feel the same way too if I were the one lying on you. Live your life and let me be. Why are you obsessed with me?

You need not guess or make up anything. I'm only asking you why? You don't need time to think about it, you'll only think of a lie. Liar.

Love letter to the moon,

I love you even though I cannot see you sometimes. I guess you are like God and you love me too. You are beautiful and mysterious. I look for you each night and I miss you when I do not see you. The sky is empty without you and so am I.
You are a glorious light, perhaps greater than I will ever realize though I try.

I want to know you more intimately, but I'm afraid we'll get too close and things will change.

There is comfort in this distance between Earth and sky and you and I.
You captivate me. You are full of wonder. Sometimes I stare at you all night not sure what I have gained but I am full after.

Sometimes I imagine us romantically, how divine, how sweet! Even the stars approve. I know you love me. I can feel it. I can tell by the way you look back at me.

Even though you do not speak, you tell me everything I want to hear.
I am yours. You have me. I mean that sincerely.
 I love you full moon. I love you crescent moon and

I enjoy your midnight kisses. I love you hot and naked honestly, but since we love each other there is no need to rush.
11/30/2013

Days

Days are the same
Betrayed body
Secrets are true
traded Security
skinned knees hurts
promises are frail
cars and bars
loved him more than me
Root deep kisses
pass all mirrors in mourning
right now I love you forever
trying to be present half a world away
heart absent, mind back in transit
I'm coming please don't leave
body obey and stay
Starting to go to numb

10/12/2013

Joy and Singing

12/20/2012

We burst into joy and singing at the unveiling our hearts. Hearts
light and free. We partake in the precious wonder of being a
child. We swim in the deep blue sea, floating on its waves
confident the tide will return us safely.

We delight in merry mornings spent skipping through the full
orchard blossoming. We celebrate the scent a sweet wind
blowing in the grass and then in our hair. We live in the days of
simple pleasures. We climb large old trees and collect their
leaves.

We sing the tales of fortune as we stroll care free through the
meadow. We name each flower one by one, knowing no two are
the same. We dance to a happy rhythm with unburden joints
ready for play swaying from side to side. We run fearless through
the blanketed fields pass the summer sun.

We welcome the darkness with the moonrise. We cheer with
voices lifted high under a star smitten sky, enjoying the smiles on
the faces of friends. We trust the divine providence of riches yet
unrealized. We anchor our hope in peace at home, solace for
sleep, faces to greet, hands to shake and hugs to hold in invited
arms.

We slowly inhale each warm day of sun, and exhale each night of
stars. We sing with jubilation, each one our own chorus of praise
for childlike happiness and all its folly. The song will never be
done nor relieved of its delight.

Walls of Silk

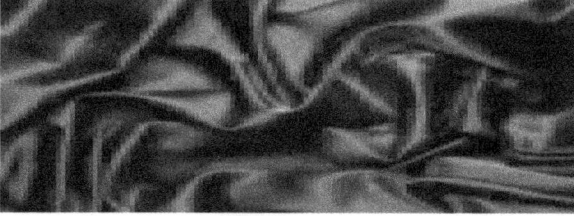

Inside these walls of silk lives a community of unity. Joined like strings of destined DNA. There is love without fear inside hearts of glass. There are mirrors that do not judge though they wear robes.

Inside these walls of silk is safety to be one's self without reservation. Imagination is god supreme. There is a feast of creativity for hungry eyes. Eyes that shine like moons and give the sky its purpose.

Human art is beautiful both bodies and minds. Naked is subjective. Diamonds do not compete. Time is suspended and passion keeps no count. There is unlimited pleasure undiscovered. Fortunes more valuable than rubies are treasured. All are welcome and free to dance as they please. The circle is open and never broken. The song never ends and the fiddle starts again.

Inside these walls of silk burns a warm fire of acceptance. Logic is uninvited. Sparks connect and give honest light. Intuition greets each guest at the door and all who crave life without limits are embraced inside these walls of silk.

Written by Alisha Ratliff as ANR 11/26/13

Inhale

4/16/2013

Oh breathe the winds of love and let them fill your soul!

Inhale and take in my sacred essence. I greet you with a warm spirit. Inhale me I pray. I bless with grace and relieve you of every worry.

I strip you of all fear and fill you with joy. Inhale new life and be richly nourished. Inhale me and be raptured in ecstasy.

Breathe deep and surrender. Love me more than kin.

Inhale me, taste my sweet body naked adorned. Touch my waiting soul with virgin lips.

Inhale me, my spirit longs to commune with you. My heart is eager to love you. Inhale me and enter my peaceful heaven.

Inhale me the way lovers do! Close your eyes see me transparently, Breathe, Breathe, Breathe!

BETRAYED

I did not see the coming nor did I hear the mumbling of your quiet betrayal.
I didn't know you weren't my friend. You only pretended to be. I did not see you pull out your knife just before you stabbed me. I didn't see your bloody smile after you'd done your deed. No, I did not see the small sprout come up after you'd planted the seed.
 I didn't know the pain I'd feel coming from my back. I did not see the damage done before my heart collapsed. I didn't see deception enter or sneak in through the cracks.
I didn't wipe the tears that welled up when I felt the sting. I did not know the dreadful harm your silent lies would bring.

I didn't know each hug and kiss were sealed with poison then. I did not see the blood drip down from where the knife went in.

I did not know so great a loss until I found the truth. I did not weep so desperately until I saw it was you.

I did not sleep. I tossed and turned wondering when and why. I did not know the grief I'd feel until I wanted to die.

I did not know you were disguised or I would have run away. I did not taste such bitter tears until I'd been betrayed.

Written by Alisha Ratliff 7/15/13

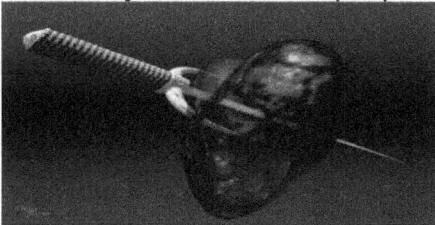

NUMB

I want to be numb, completely numb. Unconscious and unaware of any lies that would hurt me, any pain that would scar me, any judgment that would condemn me, any rejection that would trap me, and any opinion that would belittle me.
I want to be numb, completely unable to detect any feeling through the involuntary use of my senses. I don't want to think about anything. I don't care.
I just want to look. I don't want to see. I just want to swim. I don't want to breathe. I just want to listen. I don't want to hear. I just want to stare. I don't want to know. I just want to stand here. I don't want to go.
 I want to be numb.

 I don't want to feel. I don't want to say. I'll just close my eyes make it all go away. I do not want to process at all, ponder any meanings or go to any meetings. I don't want to stay. I want to be numb.

Written by Alisha Ratliff as anrcandy 7/15/13

Written by Alisha Ratliff as anr 8/9/2013

Let there be peace on earth, the peace from up above the kind that fills man's heart with love. Peace to you both enemy and friend,peace to you both stranger and kin. Peace to you both child and mother, peace to you both sister and brother.

Peace to you both lost and found. Peace to you both peasant and crowned. Peace to the sellers and peace to buyers peace to the honest and peace to the liars.

Peace to the violent.Peace to the peace keepers. Peace to the workers and the daydreamers. Peace to the women,peace to the men peace to the haters yes even peace to them.

Peace to you both daughter and son peace to the world please everyone.

Peace to the Christian peace to the Jew. Peace to the Muslim and the Hindu. Peace to the gays peace to the bis
Peace to the straights, peace to the wives.

Peace to the lockdown peace to the free peace to civilians and militaries. Peace to the right peace to the wrong. Peace to the weak peace to the strong. Peace to the dealer and peace to the user, peace to the priest and the child abuser.

Peace to the saint and peace to the sinner peace to the expert and the beginner.Peace to the old ,and peace to the young let there be peace from above to everyone.

Regret

I will not waste my time or energy on this useless epidemic regret. I refuse to cry about the past, the spilled milk of what could have been but never was.

I refuse to let it eat at me like a growing cancer infecting my soul, rehearsing the things I could've done or not done. I will not pity in the past or drown it in whiskey.

I will not second guess the conversation or anything I should've or should not have said. I will not let it spread through my body like an immortal virus. I will not take it personal or make it my fault.

Redemption and mercy share the same table with justice and regret sits in a corner alone.

I will not live in this perpetual negative consciousness punishing myself for the same crime regardless of the verdict. I will not beat the same dead horse. I simply refuse to participate.

 I take no blame undeserved, but own what is mine. I burry it and carve its name on the tombstone for all to see. I grieve the loss and leave no flowers.

I will embrace forgiveness and give myself permission to make mistakes and let live, and to love after heart break. I will give each day my very best and surrender to God all the rest.

11/26/2013

Little Girl

Little girl don't you know how precious you are?
Don't you know how beautiful you are?
You have eyes that do not sin. You are innocence
and wonder in stockings.

You have the courage and confidence of armies
without the strategy. How splendid is childlike faith.

Little girl, don't you know? This is it! Childhood is
the gift of God.
There is still time to pretend.

Imagine without worry, jump without fear, and
dream without boundaries. Eat without counting
calories, explore and do not worry about germs.
                              Play!
Enjoy today and all its delight for soon someone
will come and call you a woman.
Written by Alisha Ratliff as a in anrcandy August 9,
2013

A Woman

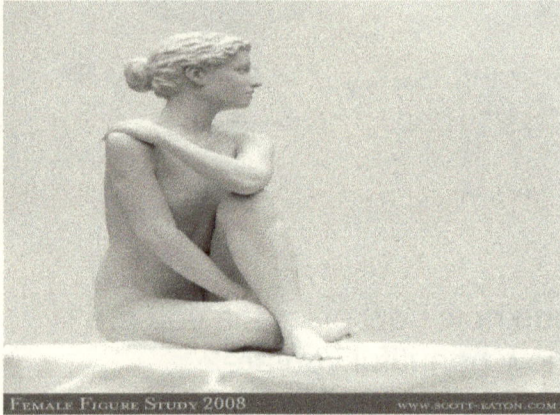

FEMALE FIGURE STUDY 2008   WWW.SCOTT-EATON.COM

A beautiful naïve girl looked into the mirror on not such a beautiful day for painful occasion.

The day she finally heard the voice of reason loudly echo, "He's not coming! He's not coming" over and over. "He's not coming." The words felt so sharp and the voice sounded so cold.
Tears began streaming down her face as she began repeating what she had heard as if it were a chant or act of breaking her will. "He's not coming, He's not coming!" she continued. The tears fell harder and faster forming a bitter stream down her neck. "He's not coming."

And in the shattering reality of that moment she became a woman.
"He's not coming. He's not coming"

12/15/2013

10/25/13

Your absence is approaching like night, dark and sure. I'm trying
to make peace with the fact that you are leaving. I know the date.
I know the time. I know it has to be this way, yet I cannot
swallow. I haven't found the room for it in my stomach. I have
no space you cannot fill.

I've told myself I'll cry no river of guilt trip tears. Nor drown in
a sea of sadness, nor make your journey bitter. No I'll find the
good in this goodbye.

In the many smiles that we shared and the meals we made, and
the time I looked into your eyes and saw love in them. Goodbye.
You will not change your mind and I will not change mine, no
even though we have second guessed this moment a thousand
times. I forbid you to stay. I will not cave in when the pain
becomes unbearable.

I will not be afraid when I call for you and remember you cannot
come. I will reach for you in the chaos and you will think of me
in the silence and we will find each other in between breathes.
I'll count this farewell fair one day in the number of hours we
have spent watching movies and laughing. When my body
contours to your arms I'll toss and turn looking for a new
comfortable. When my tears beg for your shoulders I will wipe
them and all will be well.

I am happy to wish you joy in a place I cannot be, because
friends do anything for each other and I know you would do that
for me.

I cannot stop you from taking a piece of my heart with you so I will only tell you to cherish it. And I will not grieve the memories you leave. I will celebrate them.

 I will mourn losing you with a drink in my hand toasting to new beginnings
and I'll pray this be a short forever.

Train Changer

I wish you would have waited until we'd pulled into the station before jumping off the train. At the station the train stops and people stand up and say proper goodbyes. They hug and wave and say things they weren't bold enough to say before. Some cry, some realize this is goodbye forever, but at least they do it on solid ground not a moving train swaying from side to side moving full speed ahead. They have gravity to brace them. I would have liked that for us. I considered us better.

Now don't get me wrong, I'm not upset. I did not expect you to go with me all the way to the end, but I did expect you to wait until we had pulled into the station before jumping off.

I can understand wanting to get away, changing trains and needing to go in a different direction but you left so abruptly. Your cold departure left me wondering what kind of passenger you really were.

I am grateful for the time we shared. We
got off the train together and explored
destinations that were final for some but
not for us, and so we return to the train
fuller, wiser and happier. We continued the
journey stop after stop, station after
station enjoying each experience for the
lessons in them, until somewhere along the
way you decided a departure without goodbye
was better for you. No warning, no waving,
no hugging no proper goodbye.
You leaped off suddenly and dramatically.
It seemed so easy and natural to you, but
not for me. You executed the perfect
abandonment and it was everything I hoped
it wouldn't be, painful confusing and
mysterious.
But that is life and the train continues as
if it were unconcerned or even unaware of
your decision, but I am. Here I sit still
moving full speed ahead on the train
without you, approaching a new station
where we will exchange no goodbyes and I
will continue my journey praying for the
courage to stay on the train until the
final destination. Praying I won't get off
and change trains and head back in the
opposite direction looking for a familiar
temporary.

Written by Alisha Nicole Ratliff as anr
September 26, 2013

Dear Missing Piece,

I do not understand why you have decided to just up and leave me without explanation. One minute you were here the next minute you had vanished like a monster in the closet when the lights are turned on. You did not leave a note explaining your sudden and unexpected departure or if and when you might return.

I would love to know why you left. The questions and assumptions fill my head simultaneously forcing me to play an involuntary game of mental tug of war.

Did you decide you needed a new adventure or to try someone new? Did staying become too difficult? Is this even about me?

I'm sure you would not have left if you knew how vital you were and still are. I miss you.

Whatever the reason please find a way to contact me and return.

I want you to know you have left a huge void in my soul, a deep dark hole, and I have not slept or dreamt since you left. I have not tasted or eaten. I have not felt or desired.

You are the harmonious rhythm of my heart beat, even an entire orchestra could do you no justice. You skip with me through creative spaces like happy little girls, and you race for my destiny, one greater than the sum of the galaxies.

You are the messenger running through my neurons connecting my thoughts and actions with least amount of hesitation. You are the air that refills my lungs when they collapse under the weight of another day's journey. You are the fluidity that floods my veins with serenity. You are warm and definite.

I have not been myself since you left. All that remains is a shadow where you use to be, and emptiness and pain in the space you use to fill.

This is my life as a result of your mysterious abandonment.

I'm begging you, come back to me so that I can be human again. I long for our reunion, so that I can laugh and cry and love. I anxiously await your return so that I can be whole.

Sincerely yours,

Broken

Written by: Alisha Ratliff as anr 8/16/2013

Gypsy

Please don't stone me because I did not follow the yellow brick road. Please don't condemn because I didn't take the path you wanted for me, the path of least resistance and risk. Please don't hate me because I did not turn out the way you thought. I didn't plan to be a black sheep. I tried to be "normal" honestly I did.

I know this is hard to accept. I guess I'll wear the scarlet letter and be myself authentically. This would all be easier if I just wanted what everyone else wants. I tried but my efforts failed. I pretended to but it was exhausting. That suit did not fit.
I'm not a house wife or soccer mom. I'm a gypsy, a Pisces, a free spirit. I blow with the wind and when I cannot go I wish myself there. I take my backpack and a map and I go. I take my chances.

My eulogy reads like a book of unbelievable adventures. One hundred countries, one hundred lovers, one hundred friends, ten thousand readers, one incredible life.
No mortgage, no dog, no white picket fence, no divorce, no mini-van just good old memories from a sharp mind, crazy stories and lots of books!

12/20/13

Raindrops

I hear raindrops falling on the rooftop, drops of heaven falling to earth splashing as they land. They create muddy puddles reminding man of his beginning. Drip drop drip drop. They sound like marching, like the marching of an army in perfect execution.

I hear raindrops falling to the ground. They sound like drums, like seasoned Congas beating a sweet, happy rhythm I can dance to and sway to, they play for me.

Drip drop. They sound like someone running, like a busy mother in a hurry. They sound like a soothing lullaby inviting sleep to visit tired eyes and take their rest, gently washing away the cares of the day into a sea of dreams.

I hear raindrops falling to the ground. They sound like whispers, sensual whispers bidding lovers to come and share a sexy shower.

They sound like heavy breathing, and rapid hearts beating. Drip drop they sound like lovers panting after lovemaking trying to recover from orgasmic pleasure.

I hear rain drops falling on the rooftop. Drip drop they sound like clocks, like tick tocks counting down a long work day, counting down the minutes to home.

Drip drop. They sound like children laughing as they play carefree in the park, skipping unencumbered.

I hear raindrops falling on the rooftop. Drip drop and they sing to me from heaven the raindrop song drip drop.

Written by Alisha Ratliff as anr

8/15/13